MW00564852

The Library of Future Medicine

The Revolution in Healing the Brain

JENNIFER VIEGAS

The Rosen Publishing Group, Inc.
New York

Published in 2003 by The Rosen Publishing Group, Inc.
29 East 21st Street, New York, NY 10010

Library of Congress Cataloging-in-Publication Data

Viegas, Jennifer.
The revolution in healing the brain / Jennifer Viegas.— 1st ed.
p. cm. — (The library of future medicine)
Includes bibliographical references and index.
ISBN 0-8239-3668-6
1. Brain—Juvenile literature. 2. Neurology—Juvenile literature. [1. Brain. 2. Neurology.]
I. Title. II. Series.
QP361.5 .V54 2002
612.8'2—dc21

2001006721

Manufactured in the United States of America

Cover image: Doctors Daniel Woo *(left)* and Robert Ernst read brain scans at University Hospital in Cincinnati.

Contents

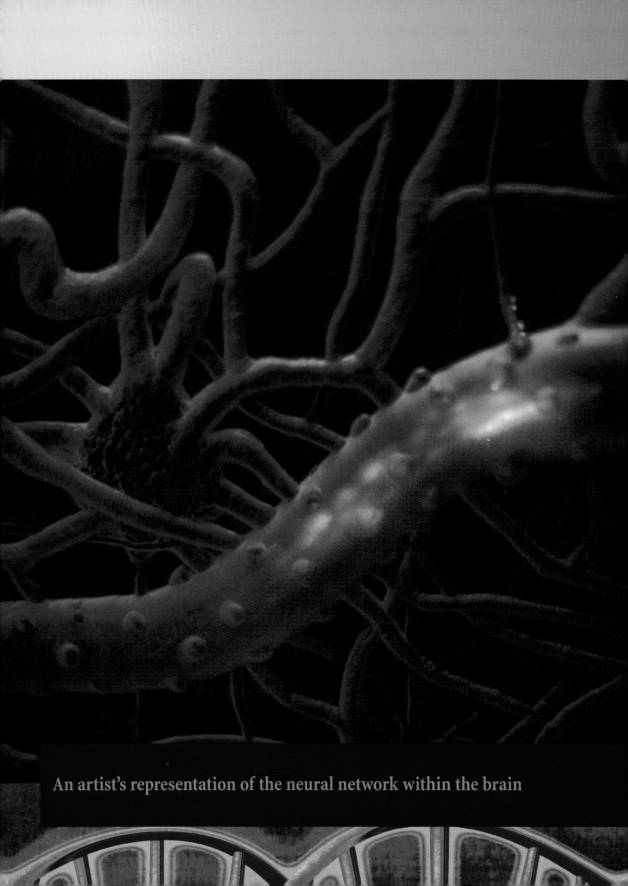

An artist's representation of the neural network within the brain

1 Brain Basics

Science allows us to understand the facts, actions, and laws that guide the world around us. Normally scientific inspection can rely upon mind over matter, but in analyzing the human brain the mind is the matter. This is the same organ that described the laws of science in the first place. Basically, the brain must figure itself out.

The brain's complexity makes it a very difficult organ to study. Only recently has technology allowed researchers to study the human brain while it is functioning. In the early days of medicine, physicians had to make educated guesses as to what parts of the brain controlled certain functions. They did this mostly by inspecting organs of people who had already died. Now high-tech imaging equipment allows researchers to study healthy people. Yet even this science is just now getting started.

The past several decades have seen many breakthroughs in brain research, and methods now exist for healing health problems that affect the

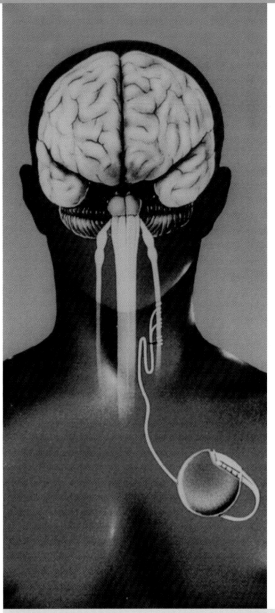

brain. An important change concerns classifying brain disorders as being true mental illnesses. In the not too distant past, individuals suffering from mental disorders were often held responsible for their condition. Earlier, it was thought that a person with chronic depression could snap out of it. Now mental health professionals realize that depression is a clinical illness that can be treated with help from therapy, pharmaceuticals, or a combination of both.

A complete map of the brain has yet to be created.

The NeuroCybernetic Prosthesis System, shown above, consists of a generator and nerve stimulator electrode that transmits electric signals to the Vagus nerve. Though currently used largely to control epileptic seizures, it has shown promising results in relieving depression.

Scientists are still trying to pinpoint precisely where specialized activities take place in the brain. It is like scanning the universe for stars. Every so often, a new star will be identified. Likewise, new areas of the brain are being discovered slowly. Such discovery, however, will open up even more questions than existed before. Just as the universe seems to be infinite, the brain also seems to possess endless capabilities.

Science is already on the threshold of cloning human brains and creating mechanical devices that can control brain function. These and other innovations could revolutionize brain research. Yet they also remind us of our own limitations. Unlocking the secrets of the brain will bring about many moral issues concerning creation and the role of science. Current and future generations must use the information wisely. We must ensure that we are controlling the technological revolution in brain research, and not the other way around. For example, artificial intelligence may one day equal, or even exceed, that of human intelligence. Already computers can design and manipulate other computers. In the wrong hands, such innovations could undermine large computerized systems, such as the Internet, or worse if applied to mind control.

The brain regulates all of the senses—sight, smell, taste, touch, and hearing. The eyes, nose, taste buds, nerves, and ears capture information about the world around us, but it is the brain that makes sense of the data. Research concerning how the brain processes sensory information may lead to improved visual and hearing aids for those who are blind or deaf. One day these conditions may even be reversible.

Memory and learning are also centered in the brain. As science reveals more about how memories are formed

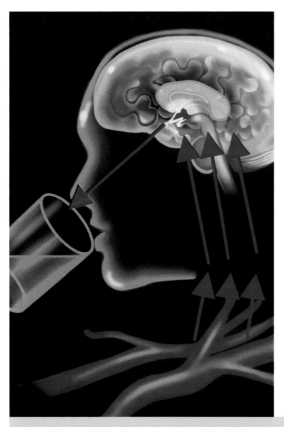

and how the brain ages, researchers move closer toward finding treatments, and possible cures, for learning disabilities and diseases like Alzheimer's, a condition that damages the brain's ability to retrieve and create memories.

One of the most promising areas of brain research involves the brain's ability to heal itself. We take for granted that other parts of

Nerve impulses from the body tell the brain that the body is dehydrated, generating the feeling of thirst.

the body can self-heal themselves. For example, a minor scratch on the skin will form a scab by itself and gradually close the wound. While the brain is not able to self-heal so quickly, recent studies suggest that the brain can reorganize itself after illness or injury. For example, the brain of a person who becomes blind after birth seems to adapt to the condition, reorganizing the parts of the brain normally involved in visual processes.

Brain research is moving at a rapid pace, thanks to computers, improved technology, and greater interest in the field. A revolution is taking place in terms of research, and this revolution will hopefully lead to more accurate diagnosis and treatment of brain disorders. With this rapid change, however, comes a larger sense of responsibility.

TREATING THE BRAIN

Before effectively treating diseases and disorders related to the brain, scientists and physicians must have a clear understanding of how the brain works. While the basics of brain function are known, researchers continue to engage in studies to better understand how each and every cell, chemical, and component operate in the brain.

You might compare brain treatment to car repair. You may have a good idea of how a car operates. Repairs such as changing the oil filter or the spark plugs are basic knowledge. But in order to repair or rebuild these parts of the car, you need to understand everything about their structure and how they relate to the other parts of the automobile. Similarly, by understanding how the brain works, researchers can affect how this organ operates. Yet they are not now at the stage where they can easily reconstruct damaged sections.

There is an interesting parallel between brain research and the computer revolution. As scientists learn more about how the brain works, computer specialists are coming closer to building computers with functions that more closely resemble human thought and activity. In fact, a computer is loosely modeled on how information travels through the brain. Electricity moving through switches on chips distributes information in a computer, while nerve impulses traveling across neuron cells in the brain control data movement.

NEURONS

A neuron is like a small piece of an electrical cord. When working together, neurons form nerves. Nerves carry messages to and from the brain. They work much the same as cords taking electricity and information to and from a computer.

Nerves work very fast, sometimes even faster than the brain. For example, you have probably at some point had a

Functional Magnetic Resonance Imaging

Improved ways for inspecting and monitoring the brain have made the healing revolution possible. One of the most promising methods for studying the brain is functional magnetic resonance imaging (fMRI). This technique allows scientists to take pictures of the brain while it is active and working. fMRI lets researchers identify which specific brain regions are involved for different tasks. All of this research happens without ever having to cut into the skull. Since analysis of each task requires a separate study, the process takes a long time. When more data from fMRIs is collected, it will be possible to draw a more complete map of the brain.

doctor test your reflexes. The doctor sharply taps you below the kneecap. This causes you to kick. The kicking action happens because the nerve cells send a signal up through the spinal cord and back to the leg muscles. Before your brain has a chance to register the impact, the leg has already tried to kick.

The neurons that make up nerves have a sleek structure that allows them to accomplish very fast messaging.

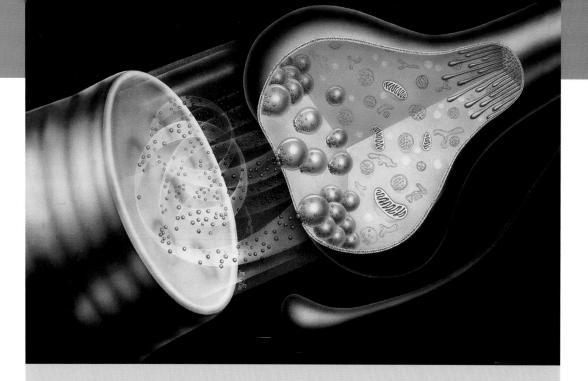

A chemical neurotransmitter crosses the synapse, or space between two neurons, to carry impulses from one neuron to the next.

Threadlike structures radiate out of the neuron's round central body. These threads are called axons and dendrites.

Axons are microscopically thin but very strong. One reason for their durability is that a fatty, insulating cover called the myelin sheath protects them. It functions like the hard plastic coating that covers most electrical cords and wires. Axons carry messages away from neurons.

Dendrites do just the opposite. They take messages to neurons. Dendrites stick out of the cell body, like fibers from a root. They are covered with a protective myelin sheath that both protects and aids in the transmission of nerve impulses. Myelin is an electrical insulator. It helps to speed up conduction.

SYNAPSE

Models of the human brain suggest that it is a solid object. In truth, the neurons that make up the brain do not even touch each other. A tiny space, called a synapse, separates one neuron from another. Messages coming to and from a neuron must pass across this gap.

Chemicals are the means by which the information is communicated. When a message coded within an electrical impulse reaches an axon, the electricity causes the cell to release a chemical, called a nerve transmitter substance, or a neurotransmitter. When impulses reach a synapse, the neurotransmitters pour out of the sending cell through an axon. The substance then suddenly leaps across the synapse where it reaches dendrites on the next neuron. The dendrite then releases its own electrical impulse. The process continues in a chain reaction until the message reaches its final destination. It takes only about three one-thousandths of a second for a nerve impulse to travel from one cell to another.

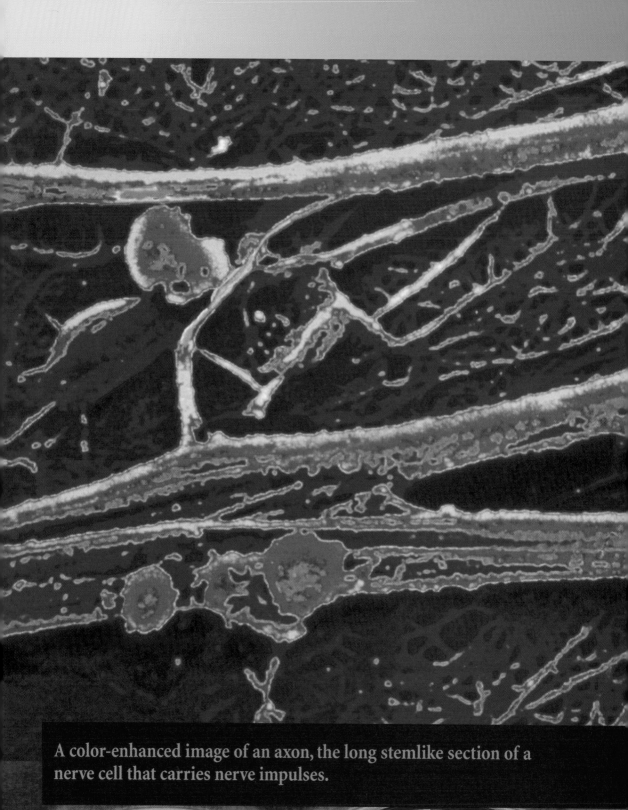

A color-enhanced image of an axon, the long stemlike section of a nerve cell that carries nerve impulses.

Chemical Disorders and Treatments

Several kinds of chemicals travel from neuron to neuron. In a healthy person, these chemicals are perfectly balanced. Some people, however, have too much, or too little, of a certain chemical. This can create a chemical imbalance. Such an imbalance can affect a person's health, mood, and behavior. Depression and anxiety disorders have been linked to chemical imbalances within the brain.

DEPRESSION

Clinical depression is very different from normal sadness. It is often hard to diagnose because its early symptoms are so similar to ordinary reactions to distressing situations. After a certain period of time, however, mental health professionals can determine whether the sadness is normal or a sign of depression.

Symptoms, however, can vary from person to person. Some people can function at a seemingly normal level, revealing little of their feelings to outsiders.

Others may cry for no apparent reason and have trouble even getting out of bed in the mornings. If left untreated, the person may never reach his or her full potential. Tragically, some people act on their thoughts of suicide.

CAUSES OF DEPRESSION

Depression has been associated with two sets of chemicals within the brain: autoreceptors and transporters. They regulate the movement of nerve signals, present in neurotransmitters, from neuron to neuron in the brain. Autoreceptors communicate with neurons, telling them to stop releasing neurotransmitters when the time is right. Transporters then have the job of returning some of the neurotransmitters back to the neuron from which they originated. Because there are millions of neurons and several different types of neurotransmitters, the process is complex and can be thrown off balance.

People with depression often do not release sufficient amounts of neurotransmitters. Another problem may be that the return of the neurotransmitter back to the originating neuron, a process called reuptake, is irregular. In clinical depression, three neurotransmitters likely are affected: dopamine, norepinephrine, and serotonin.

TREATING DEPRESSION

Great strides have been made in treating depression. A few decades ago, most patients were advised to undergo therapy. Therapy is still advised, but research has led the way to new and improved antidepressant medications. At present, most of these drugs fall under the general description of selective serotonin reuptake inhibitors (SSRIs). Trial and error has shown that regulation of serotonin seems to control depression, while causing the least amount of side effects.

SSRIs stop transporters from carrying through with reuptake.

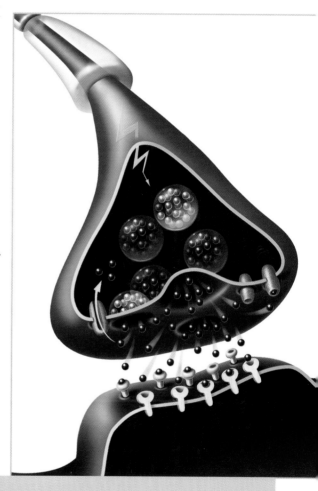

At the synapse, the tiny space between nerve cells, neurotransmitter chemicals are released that trigger impulses between nerve cells.

They prevent the transporters from returning the extra neurotransmitter chemicals to the original neuron. In depressed individuals, the reuptake process seems to cause a buildup of chemicals in the system. Four widely prescribed SSRIs are Luvox, Paxil, Prozac, and Zoloft. Although they have side effects, studies have shown that these are minimal when compared to the side effects of earlier antidepressants. And these side effects are better than the effects of depression itself.

Much more needs to be learned about depression and the interactions between autoreceptors and transporters. As science reveals more about these issues, pharmaceutical companies will be able to develop better treatments for depression with few, to zero, side effects.

ANXIETY DISORDERS

There are several different kinds of anxiety disorders. Three of the most common are generalized anxiety disorder, panic disorder, and phobia.

Sadness is a normal reaction to events that disturb us. Anxiety is also an ordinary feeling that we all experience at times. In fact, it is one of our tools for survival. When the body senses danger, a "fight or flight" response often kicks in, causing us to flee from the threat.

 Drug and Alcohol Abuse

Long-term use of intoxicants such as alcohol and illegal drugs can cause changes to the brain. Studies of the effects of cocaine use, for example, reveal modifications in the strength of neural connections in the brain. These connections are most often associated with feelings of pleasure. In addition to causing addiction, cocaine appears to cause brain alterations that last long after the drug is used. Similar findings have been documented for methamphetamines. Chronic alcohol abuse can produce similar effects, with some alcoholics showing damage to, or loss of, cell tissue in the cortex and other brain regions.

A person with generalized anxiety disorder (GAD) cannot associate his or her fear with a specific event, object, or situation. Feelings of fear are present for no apparent reason. GAD sufferers may experience rapid heart rates, hyperactivity, trouble sleeping, and fatigue.

Panic disorder is characterized by the occurrence of panic attacks. Attacks can be triggered by events, based on past bad experiences, or they may be unpredictable. Victims may feel shortness of breath, rapid heart rates, sweating, nausea, or a combination of all of these symptoms.

Phobias range from minor to major. Most people report having some kind of phobia. It could be a fear of heights or of spiders, for example. Agoraphobia, which often happens with panic attacks, causes the victim to fear open spaces. Many agoraphobics have trouble traveling or even leaving their own homes.

CAUSES OF ANXIETY DISORDERS

Similar to depression, anxiety disorder is believed to develop when autoreceptors and transporters are not working properly. In this case, the neurotransmitter adrenaline is thought to be the primary chemical involved. Also, there appears to be a genetic basis for panic problems. Individuals with serious anxiety conditions usually report having at least one other immediate family member with a similar disorder.

TREATING ANXIETY DISORDERS

Treatments for anxiety disorders vary, depending on which type of anxiety disorder has been identified. For someone with a simple phobia, mental health professionals can usually desensitize the person to the feared object or event by gradual, repeated exposure. As the patient becomes more at ease, the fear gradually goes away.

Treatment for more severe cases often involves cognitive therapy and anxiety-reducing drugs, such as monoamine oxidase inhibitors, which prevent decomposition of certain neurotransmitters, and tricyclic antidepressants. These antidepressants increase levels of neurotransmitters, most often serotonin, in the brain. Certain brain chemicals linked to anxiety, such as serotonin, are also involved in depression.

NEURON DISORDERS

Medical specialists now have a better understanding of diseases that can affect neurons. Parkinson's and Alzheimer's are two common diseases that may impair brain function.

Parkinson's sufferers can experience tremors, difficulty speaking, and problems in moving their arms and/or legs. They are lacking the chemical dopamine, which helps to transfer electrical impulses across neurons. In most cases, it appears that the neurons that create dopamine deep within the brain are either damaged or destroyed.

Alzheimer's patients have trouble remembering things. Over time their memories progressively worsen. As the disease follows its deadly course, sufferers may lose the ability to recognize familiar places and even family members. They can require constant care and may become vulnerable to infections like pneumonia.

The brain of an Alzheimer's victim contains abnormal amounts of plaque made up of a protein called amyloid-beta. The plaque groupings are surrounded by damaged and dead neurons. In severe cases, patients will even be unable to use entire sections of their brains, which have been overcome by the plaque.

HOPE FOR NEURON DISORDERS

While there still is no clinically proven way to prevent or cure diseases like Parkinson's and Alzheimer's, scientists are hopeful that exciting new research using stem cells can restore damaged or missing neurons.

STEM CELLS

Stem cells are cells that divide and reproduce themselves for an indefinite amount of time. Nurtured in a laboratory setting, the cells may be transformed into virtually any type of cell found within the human body.

Researchers now are primarily focusing on two types of stem cells: human embryonic stem cells and adult human bone marrow stem cells. Scientists already have turned

A doctor records her observations as she leads her patient through a series of tests for Parkinson's disease.

embryonic stem cells, or cells derived from human embryos, into brain cells. The laboratory brain cells were implanted into rodent brains, where they developed into healthy, functioning neurons.

Controversy surrounds the use of embryonic stem cells, which must be taken from discarded human embryos, so researchers are also working with adult human bone marrow stem cells. These stem cells have the ability to take the form of many types of human body cells, including brain neurons. In laboratory tests, bone marrow stem cells have, through combinations of certain growth factors and nutrients, been

Theory Behind Alzheimer Cell Death

A protein in the brain, amyloid precursor protein (APP), generates the plaque-forming amyloid-beta. Proteins are difficult for scientists to analyze because of their complexity. For many years, it was not clear how this plaque clogged up brain pathways and led to cell death. Now recent studies suggest that a bio-chemical reaction takes place between APP and an enzyme involved in moving signals and other materials across axons.

When the reaction takes place and plaque has formed, axon pathways appear to suffer a blockage. Information about the clogged axon is passed to the neuron. While the exact cause of nerve cell death remains unknown, some researchers theorize that the clogged axons create signals that cause the neuron to die.

transformed into brain cells. Aside from avoiding controversy, human bone marrow stem cells will one day allow a patient to be his or her own donor. This lessens the risk of rejection once the newly formed neurons are implanted into the brain.

For a long time it was thought that once a person was brain damaged or suffered from a disease like Alzheimer's, there was no way of restoring brain function. Now there is hope that stem cells can be used to replace the damaged or destroyed neurons. Since stem cells reproduce themselves, it may only take a small amount of them to repair an entire brain.

CLONING

Cloning is like large-scale stem cell research. In the case of stem cells, individual cells are duplicated and used to grow specific cells. For cloning, entire living beings are copied. Scientists already have the ability to clone humans. Political and religious issues, however, have stopped cloning for now. If allowed to proceed in a carefully controlled, humane manner, cloning may enable researchers to clone full body parts. This is science fiction at present, but technology is moving toward a day when a person could replace a damaged organ with an identical lab-grown organ.

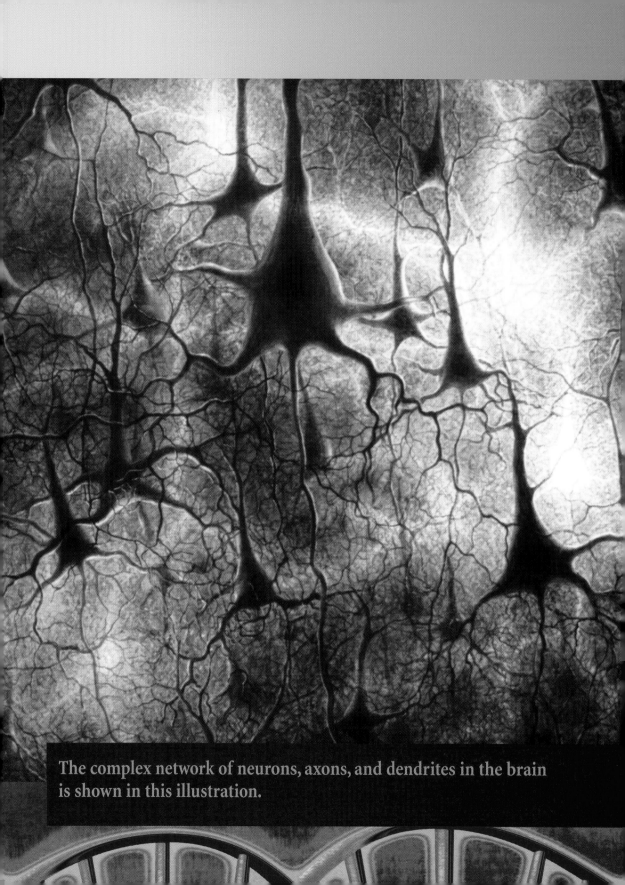

The complex network of neurons, axons, and dendrites in the brain is shown in this illustration.

Learning and Intelligence

Many researchers now are analyzing how memory, learning, and intelligence operate. Although the basics have been known for years, many questions remain unanswered about the precise mechanics. All of us can benefit from such research. No one has perfect intelligence or memory. Individuals suffering from learning disorders and conditions like Alzheimer's and Parkinson's will especially benefit. Once memory is fully understood, treatments can be designed to cure the causes and effects of these conditions.

MEMORY

The brain stores gathered information as memory. Scientists believe that the brain does this by creating unique pathways along groups of neurons. One neuron can connect with 10,000 others, so any number of routes is possible. It is almost like playing the lottery. There are a limited amount of numbers but many different combinations that the numbers can make.

Memory pathways are almost like mini road maps in the brain. When you get on a bike, for example, your brain arranges the instructions necessary for riding the bike. Every skill, from taking a shower to making a bed, requires that your neurons line up in just the right way to allow you to recall the appropriate instructions.

A doctor watches as her patient completes a memory test.

It is amazing how accurate the brain is at pulling out the right brain map. You do not even have to shuffle through sets of memories, as a computer would have to, in order to choose the right one. In a split second your brain accesses the correct set of instructions.

IMMEDIATE AND WORKING MEMORY

There are three basic types of memory: immediate, working, and long-term. We

g Memory

erm memory? Some people
n others. Much of this is sim-
re attention. A person with
us on the task at hand and
and things that might be

u to test your short-term mem-
he list below for thirty sec-
, look away, and see how
mber:
ter, skateboard, dog, pizza,
magazine, train, window,

immediate memory. It lasts for only an instant. An example of immediate memory is how we process images viewed on film. Gaps occur as one still image moves to the next. Our brain registers these gaps, but then puts the images together to form a moving scene.

Working memory operates similar to RAM (random access memory) on a computer. Information is stored for a limited period of time before it can be erased. While the human brain may never totally erase anything, it does put some things into a sort of recycling bin that does not get much use. For example, at some point you have probably been given a telephone number that you forgot almost as soon as it was told to you.

Working memory holds only about seven items at a time. They can be words, pictures, numbers, letters, faces, or anything that you see, hear, or experience in your environment. Working memory lasts for about a minute.

LONG-TERM MEMORY

Long-term memory can last anywhere from a few minutes to many years. People in their eighties can often remember things that happened when they were small children. You already have a lot of information stored in your long-term memory. Years from now, you may even be able to remember reading this book and what you learned from it.

It is estimated that the human brain can store 100 trillion pieces of information. The brain, however, is much more efficient than a computer or filing cabinet. You do not have 100 trillion maps floating around in your head, only the tiny codes that let your brain reconstruct certain memory pathways.

Scientists are not completely certain why some things go into long-term memory while others do not. For example, you can probably remember something seemingly unimportant that you did several years ago. Most long-term memories, however, form when the brain uses a particular road map of mental connections over and over again. Similar to exercising a muscle, the brain is then able to strengthen and reinforce certain neural connections, which imprints the map as memory. We also tend to remember important things, such as events that have a lasting impact on our lives.

INTELLIGENCE

Intelligence is a measure of a person's ability to judge, comprehend, and reason. Many factors determine a person's intelligence. A number of recent studies suggest that intelligence is inherited. Parents may not only contribute to obvious traits such as height and hair color but also to personality traits and brain power.

Some studies of twins reveal that brain regions controlling language and reading skills are virtually the same among identical twins who share the same genes. Siblings who were raised in a similar manner, but who possessed different genes, displayed far more brain differences. This genetic link suggests that a predisposition to brain diseases, such as schizophrenia and dementia, can be inherited. It also provides evidence that an individual's intelligence quotient (IQ) may be predictable, based upon the IQ of the parents. With hard work, however, most healthy individuals have a good chance to succeed and to improve, no matter what the measurement is of their intelligence.

LEARNING DISABILITIES

Some people suffer from permanent or temporary learning disabilities. They have trouble with a specific skill involved in learning, such as concentration, coordination, memory, or language. Such individuals, however, may be highly intelligent.

Language problems are fairly common. An individual with this disorder may have no trouble processing ideas captured from experience or visual images. However, the person may have difficulty decoding words in his or her brain. Words may zip through your brain, with their meanings being deciphered instantaneously. For a person with a language problem, the brain gets confused when trying to figure out what the words mean.

There are many other kinds of learning disabilities. Dysphasia is a condition that impairs a person's ability to produce or understand speech. Dysgraphia affects a person's ability to write. Dyslexia interferes with a person's ability to understand both printed and spoken words. Many dyslexics have trouble with the order of letters within words or numbers within math problems. These are just a few common learning disabilities.

Science is getting better at determining what causes learning disabilities. Most researchers believe that a number of different factors are involved, including minor brain damage, chemical imbalances, neuron disorders, and problems during childhood that may prevent proper mental growth and development.

There are many treatments available to help those who have a learning disability. Treatments may include participating in special education classes, using medication, and undergoing counseling. Some educational computer programs and lesson plans even help such individuals to "rewire" their brains. This means that the information that may have been improperly stored to memory the first time can be replaced with proper information and skills.

THE AGING BRAIN

Most of us know that the body changes as a person ages. Steps are often taken to prevent the effects of aging. Lotions are used to smooth out wrinkles. Exercise and diet become more important. But what is done to help the brain combat aging? Until recently, little thought went into this subject. With a better understanding of the brain's aging process comes hope for methods of maintaining good brain function throughout our entire lives.

THE PEDIATRIC BRAIN

Functional magnetic resonance imaging in the past decade has allowed researchers to study the active brains of healthy children for the first time. Other imaging techniques required test subjects to undergo invasive procedures (operations) or to sit still for long periods of time.

Recently scientists performed fMRIs on both adults and children, testing how their brains responded to verbal quizzes. The tests were not hard, and all study participants were able to answer the questions. However, the children and the adults seemed to use different brain strategies to perform the same task. Children, for example, seemed to use their visual regions more, while adults tapped into memory centers toward the front part of the brain.

Such studies are important, not only in determining how the brain ages but also in improving our understanding of how a child's brain operates. A child that experiences a neurological disease or injury may need different treatment than an adult with the same injury. As research in this field continues, hopes rise for better treatments, and possible cures, for pediatric brain disorders.

THE SENIOR BRAIN

Between the ages of fifty and ninety, our brains begin to show significant signs of aging. The brain actually decreases in size. For example, a fifty-year-old's brain weighs approximately 3 pounds, but by the age of sixty-five, the brain has slimmed down to 2.6 pounds. Thankfully, this is believed not to result from cell death but rather from water loss in neurons.

One of the greatest changes occurs in the frontal lobe region of the brain. This area decreases in size an average of 30 percent from the age of fifty to ninety. Because the frontal lobes are associated with social and emotional responses, the decrease could explain why some older individuals have a decreased ability to control concentration, to control impulses, and to perform complex tasks. Complex tasks are believed to be affected because the change in the frontal lobes causes difficulty in focusing on several things at one time.

Additionally, brain activity slows down. This particularly becomes evident when a person tries to do several things at one time. Younger individuals seem to have less trouble performing multiple tasks than older people. Recent studies suggest that metabolism in the brain changes myelin and other chemicals, which results in a structural slowdown. Neuron connections that form memory also weaken. This makes it harder to tap into short- and long-term memories.

Blood Vessels Affect Memory

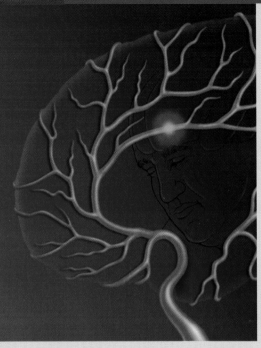

As highlighted in orange in this illustration, a stroke occurs when a small blood vessel in the brain ruptures or becomes clogged.

Blood vessels play a vital role in keeping the brain healthy. Usually doctors only detect blood vessel damage in the brain when there is a problem, such as a stroke. When a major stroke occurs, usually a large blood vessel in the brain has become blocked or ruptured. A stroke victim can suffer loss of movement, speech, and other brain functions as a result. Minor damage to blood vessels, however, may cause memory decline and balance problems. This damage may not always be evident to the patient. Now that the importance of blood vessels has been documented, researchers hope to prevent damage to them much in the same way that certain heart diseases are treated.

COMBATING THE EFFECTS OF AGING

In the past, it was accepted that age led to a natural decrease in brain function. It was just something people had to cope with. Now researchers are working on ways to fight the aging process in the brain.

Several studies are looking at how the stress hormone cortisol affects brain metabolism and function. Some scientists believe that the hormone builds up in the system, similar to how adrenaline builds up in the bodies of individuals suffering from panic disorder. Now that the problem has been identified, there is hope that drugs will soon be available to prevent problems related to cortisol.

It is also becoming more evident that with the brain, you use it or you lose it. We take this for granted with other parts of the body. If a person is sedentary for a long time, it is expected that the muscles will grow weaker and less flexible. Though not constructed of muscle tissue, the brain also requires exercise. Sadly, many seniors lose friends and relatives over the years. With such losses, their opportunity for using vital social skills drops off. An active mind is a healthy mind. That makes using our brains important for all of us, especially seniors. We must always continue learning, sharpening our memories, and participating in social activities throughout our lives.

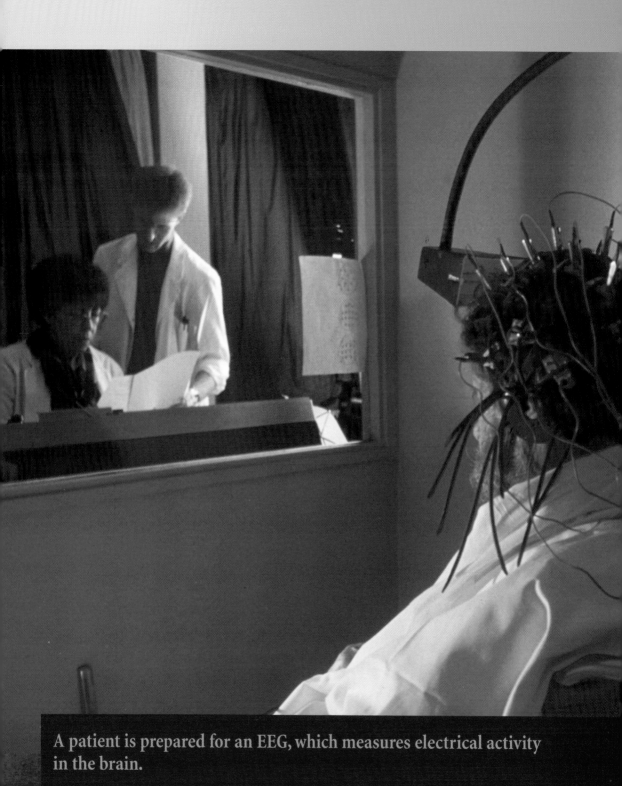

A patient is prepared for an EEG, which measures electrical activity in the brain.

4 ⟩ Sleep and Dreams

Despite years of research, many questions remain unanswered about sleep. What is clear is that sleep plays a role in both brain health and the well-being of the entire body. For example, you may stay up all night studying for an exam. In the morning, you may feel that you are not functioning at a high level, especially when compared with someone who studied and then got a good night's rest.

The importance and meaning of dreams is also not yet fully understood. Lately, though, some important breakthroughs are taking place. Researchers have been able to decipher the dreams of rodents while they were sleeping. Rodents who spent all day running through test mazes were found to dream about the activity at night. Scientists were able to figure this out by matching and comparing brain waves known to go with certain activities.

Such research is twofold. It could lead to cures for sleep disorders and recommendations for improving

Measuring Brain Waves

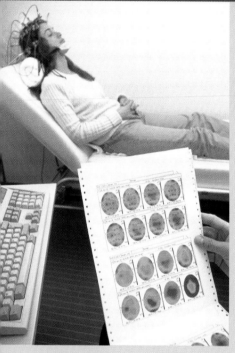

The EEG is used to help diagnose the presence and type of degenerative diseases, contusions, seizures, tumors, and other disorders that affect the brain.

Neurons in the brain actually give off measurable amounts of electricity. This electricity can be measured using a device called an electroencephalograph (EEG).

Electrodes that pick up electrical waves are attached to a person's head. The waves are processed by the machine and can be seen as lines on a computer screen or a printout on a piece of paper. When a person is awake, the EEG line looks pretty even, with small V-shaped waves of activity. During REM and deep sleep, the waves of activity occur less often, creating big V-shaped waves on the EEG line.

sleep patterns. On a more science-fiction level, deciphering the thoughts and dreams of animals could one day permit scientists to read our thoughts in real time. This could dramatically change psychotherapy and brain analysis.

BRAIN FUNCTION DURING SLEEP

During sleep, the brain moves through different levels of consciousness, or states of awareness. These are called sleep cycles. Each cycle lasts for about 80 to 120 minutes. One of the most important cycles is called rapid eye movement (REM) sleep. Dreams occur during REM sleep.

DREAMS

About ninety minutes after you go to sleep, you enter REM sleep and begin to dream. The reason it is called rapid eye movement is because your eyes really do dart back and forth under your eyelids as you dream. Dreams can contain virtually anything stored in your short- and long-term memories. While there often does not seem to be any rhyme or reason to dreaming, researchers are now finding out that dreams are very important to maintaining good mental health. It is theorized that dreams help us to process emotions and memories.

It also appears that sleep may even determine what we store to memory. During the day, we take in many different bits of information, but only some of these can be remembered at a later date. Dreams may be a way of sorting out what is worth saving and what should be tossed out.

SLEEP DISORDERS

Occasionally we all miss a few hours of sleep. At other times we might oversleep. People that have sleep disorders suffer from either of these conditions on a regular basis. Both can cause health problems. People who fall asleep uncontrollably suffer from narcolepsy. People who have trouble falling asleep suffer from insomnia.

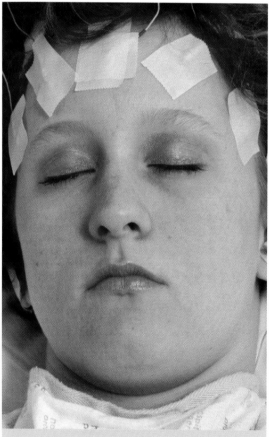

A young woman has the electrical activity in her brain measured during her sleep.

Narcolepsy is a disorder that can lead to sudden, uncontrollable moments of sleep lasting from about five to twenty minutes. A narcoleptic may fall asleep anywhere at any time, even during the middle of a conversation. Unlike healthy individuals, narcoleptics seem to go directly into REM sleep, instead of gradually entering that state. Narcoleptics are treated with medication.

Insomnia is a much more common disorder with many different possible causes. Sometimes people have trouble sleeping properly after a traumatic event or some other kind of stressful situation. In this case, stress signals released by the cerebral cortex are stuck in an "on" position. The brain stem never gets the message that it is OK to fall asleep. Other causes for insomnia include illness, such as asthma and high blood pressure. Consumption of stimulants, like caffeine found in soda and coffee, also cause sleeplessness.

RESULTS OF INSOMNIA

A few sleepless nights will probably just leave you feeling tired and worn out. You may have trouble remembering and focusing on things. Even twenty-four hours without sleep can lead to such symptoms.

After approximately ten days without sufficient sleep, a person may not be able to think clearly. Hallucinations and other signs of mental illness can occur. Clearly, getting a good night's sleep is essential to maintaining both emotional and physical health. Studies in the future are likely to reveal more about the importance of sleep and dreams in maintaining proper brain function.

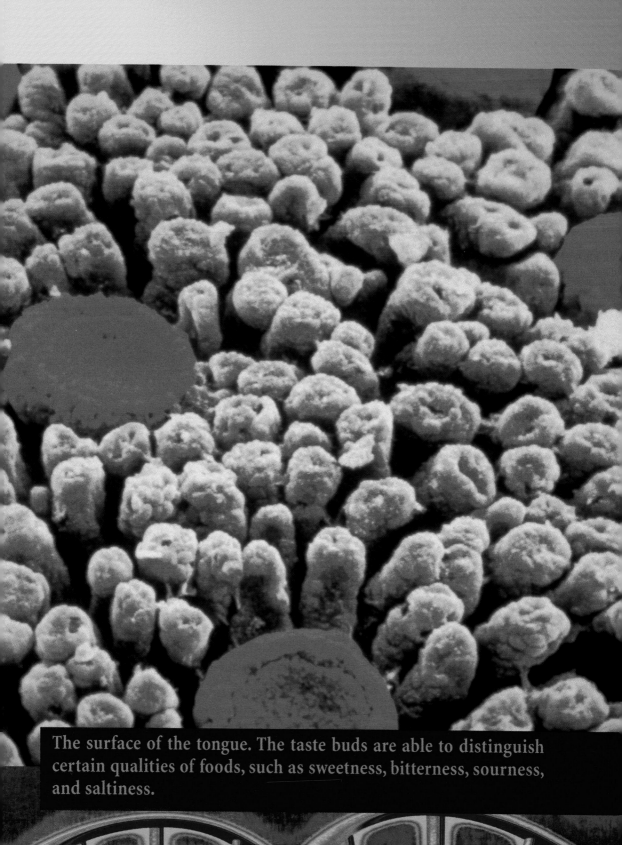

The surface of the tongue. The taste buds are able to distinguish certain qualities of foods, such as sweetness, bitterness, sourness, and saltiness.

5 ▷ Sensory Awareness

Sensory awareness would not be possible without the brain. Each of the five senses—sight, touch, taste, hearing, and smell—relies upon the brain's ability to gather and process data from the outside world. Scientific breakthroughs in understanding how the senses work are paving the way for treatments to come in the years ahead.

HOW BRAIN RESEARCH AIDS VISION DISORDERS

Because the brain is so crucial to the vision process, an individual could possess two perfect eyes and yet still be blind. This is because a problem within the brain could somehow disrupt the transfer of image information from the eyes to the visual cortices.

A few decades ago, most neuroscientists believed that the brain had an extremely limited ability to adapt to injury or disease. This included conditions that lead to blindness after birth or in adulthood. Now researchers are disc ̶ering that people who lose their sight early in life show evidence of brain reorganization. With severe sight loss and blindness, the visual cortex region of the brain is no longer used to process data coming in from the eyes. Recent studies suggest that this seemingly idle region in blind individuals is utilized for other sensory awareness tasks, such as hearing and smell. The brain seems to sharpen other senses to make up for what is lost.

In the future, this finding may lead to improved therapies for the blind, and perhaps even the ability to reverse the condition. One biotechnology company already has developed a microchip that replaces degenerated nerve cells in the eye that transmit visual information to the brain. Studies are still being conducted before the device is implanted in humans.

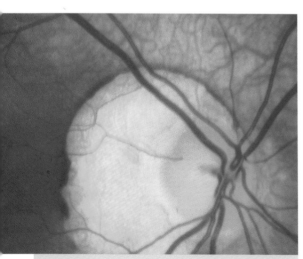

The human optic nerve

Other problems, such as dyslexia, could have their origins within the brain. Since dyslexics sometimes see words and numbers backward, there may be a problem with how neuron pathways are formed in the brain. In many cases, it is possible to "rewire" the brain, through special education exercises, to improve the condition.

HOPE FOR THE HEARING IMPAIRED

As with blindness, people may become deaf as a result of any number of brain disorders. And in the same way that a person might adapt to blindness, evidence exists that a deaf individual adapts to the condition by using the auditory cortex to perceive data other than direct sound, such as vibrations resulting from sound waves. The brain's ability to "rewire" itself holds promise that a cure for deafness may be possible in the future.

SMELL

The sense of smell may be more important to us than we now realize. For example, researchers continue to study pheromones. Pheromones are hormonal chemicals that we all release to identify ourselves. As studies continue to reveal more about how the brain processes olfactory information, scientists will better understand how the sense of smell influences our lives.

TASTE

The senses of taste and smell are linked to emotions. For example, if you smell a favorite food, it might bring back pleasant memories. Sometimes people get addicted to food and the feelings it can release. By further studying the brain and how it operates, researchers may be able to curb this

Symphony Conductors Develop a Heightened Sense of Hearing

Conductors must listen to dozens of different instruments one at a time, yet they also listen to sounds produced by the whole symphony. During rehearsals, a conductor has the amazing ability to identify one bad sound out of a group of many different noises. How is this possible?

Scientists have determined that conductors develop keen peripheral hearing, meaning that they can better differentiate (separate) sounds that fall outside of normal boundaries. For example, if a trumpet player hits a wrong note, it will stand out amongst the other sounds that the conductor expects to hear.

kind of addiction and other emotional disorders relating to food consumption. In fact, recent studies suggest that overeating and the lack of feeling satisfied may be tied to hormonal imbalances in the body and chemical imbalances within the brain. Just as depression and anxiety disorders are viewed as medical conditions, obesity now is more accepted as being a medical disorder.

TOUCH

When you touch something very hot, you immediately pull away. You can thank the pain receptors for helping you prevent a bad burn. Pain receptors relay messages in a flash to the thalamus and the cerebral cortex in the brain. In this case, the pain serves as a helpful warning.

Stem cell research is moving toward cures for individuals who have lost movement and the sense of touch as a result of paralysis and other medical conditions. Scientists already have regenerated damaged nerve connectors in animals using lab-made nerves taken from stem cells. It is only a matter of time before this technology is applied to humans. Surgical implants could someday reverse the effects of paralysis.

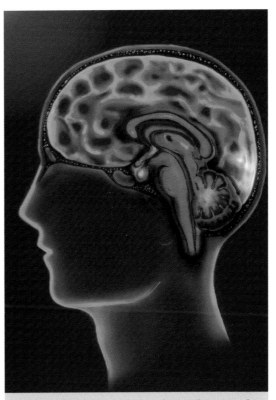

Sight disorders are often the result of disruptions in the transfer of image information between the brain and the eye.

"Jerry," who is blind, gains some vision with the help of the computer gear on his hip and a tiny camera wired to his brain. He now can read large letters and navigate around large objects in a room.

Approaching the Age of Mind Control

Technological and biotechnological innovations have helped to fuel the present revolution in healing the brain. These include functional magnetic resonance imaging and high-powered microscopes, stem cell research, and better pharmaceuticals. However, there are still many unsolved mysteries. Science has yet to completely understand how the brain operates. No one has come close to creating a form of artificial intelligence that matches human mind power, but if research continues at its present pace, the day will come when computer technology can mimic brain function.

VIRTUAL REALITIES

Already NASA researchers have developed a technology that joins the human nervous system with computers. The device is an armband implanted with electrodes. It allows its wearers to control external equipment using hand gestures. In the future, this may allow surgeons to perform delicate procedures without touching the patient.

The Brain's Complexity

Doctors have created artificial hearts, limbs, and other part of the body. The brain, for now, is a product of creation and not science. As a measurement of the brain's complexity, consider that there are one hundred billion neurons in the brain. The brain packs an incredible amount of processing power into a very small space. The number of synapses is also staggering. A baby has fifty trillion, but during the first month of life this figure jumps to one quadrillion.

Using the same basic technology, researchers also are planning to use human brainwaves to control external devices. In studies individuals with electrodes attached to the sides of their heads have moved objects by thought. A person can imagine moving an object to the left or right and, without touching it directly, enable the movement through a device that has received and decoded the brain-wave controls.

THOUGHT-CONTROLLED COMPUTERS

In recent years, scientists have discovered a lot about how the brain works and how we think. A few patients with brain damage already have been helped by electrodes implanted in their heads that help to control their brain functions. Neurons in the brains of these individuals activated the electrodes, which were connected to a computer. Over time the patients were able to learn which thoughts produced certain outcomes on the computer.

COMPUTERIZED BRAINS

If the brain can control a computer, then it is likely that computers will one day be able to control the human brain. In fact, a pair of married researchers in England has devised a system whereby one individual can control specific movements in the second individual. A surgically implanted silicon chip in one person, with a built-in power source, tuner, and radio receiver, communicates with a surgically implanted chip inserted in the brain of the other person to receive the signals.

At first this technology might seem like a novelty, but it may one day lead to a cure for paralysis and other mobility disorders. For example, a person with a spinal cord injury may one day be able to relay his or her brain signals through a computer chip, eliminating the need for neuron transmission down the spinal cord. If nerves are still intact in the limbs, the signal could allow for movement, just as nerve impulses do in healthy individuals.

The renowned theoretical physicist Stephen Hawking suffers from amyotrophic lateral sclerosis, a type of motor disorder in which brain cells that control movement progressively die, causing muscles to atrophy. Hawking is able to communicate through a computer and a speech synthesizer.

HOLDING THE FUTURE IN OUR HANDS

If robotic brains move from the realm of science fiction into reality, life as we now know it could change forever. A hint at what might occur comes from research on computer design. Scientists recently developed an integrated software system that enables a computer to design other computers. The good news is that this could create a near-perfect computer, free from imperfections. It could also eliminate the hands-on testing of products and speed up technological innovations.

Also, as artificial intelligence and robots come closer to equaling, or perhaps even exceeding, human brain power, the line of control may become blurred enough that the technology itself could dictate future change. There are additional moral, political, and ethical obstacles to face, such as those seen in the debates surrounding stem cell research and cloning. These issues will, no doubt, weigh heavily on present and future generations.

UNTAPPED POWERS

Robotic brains are left to scientific debate. For now, researchers continue to study the human brain. With each day come surprising discoveries that show us just how remarkable this organ is. Future experiments will help scientists and doctors understand how to heal the brain when it is not well.

Many experts believe that today humans use only 15 percent of their brainpower. This raises the question of what is our true intellectual potential. We have already sent explorers into space and created high-tech computers. Only time will tell what lies in store for the future. Given the apparent limitless potential of the brain, the possibilities seem endless.

Glossary

auditory cortex The part of the brain that deals with processing sound.

autoreceptors Chemicals that communicate with neurons, telling them to stop releasing neurotransmitter signals when the time is right.

axon A long, threadlike part of a neuron that carries signals along the nerve cell.

brain A collected mass of nerve cells that serves as the control center of the body.

brain chemicals Substances produced by the brain that affect everything from moods to nerves. People suffering from a chemical imbalance have either too much or too little of certain brain chemicals.

brain stem The lower part of the brain that controls most vital bodily functions.

cerebral cortex The wrinkled outer covering of the cerebrum.

cerebrum The main part of the brain. It is divided into two halves, or hemispheres.

dendrite A thin extension of a neuron that carries signals to the nerve cell.

functional magnetic resonance imaging A medical imaging process that lets scientists take pictures of the brain while it is in the act of processing information (thinking).

lobe   A region in the brain; there are four main lobes in the cerebrum: the temporal, parietal, occipital, and frontal lobes.

long-term memory   Remembered things or events, usually of an important nature, that can be recalled for a long time.

myelin sheath   Fatty insulation that covers and protects neuron axons.

neuron   A nerve cell; neurons working together make up nerves.

neurotransmitters   Chemicals that carry signals from neuron to neuron.

REM sleep   Rapid eye movement sleep; a stage when the eyes twitch and dreams occur.

stem cells   Cells that divide, or reproduce themselves, for indefinite periods of time. Grown in a laboratory setting, the cells may be transformed into virtually any type of cell found within the human body.

synapse   The small space between neurons. It is here that a nerve cell exchanges information with another nerve cell.

thalamus   Located under the cerebrum and over the hypothalamus, this part of the brain helps to control sensory awareness and the muscles.

transporters   Chemicals that return neurotransmitter signal chemicals back to the neuron from which they originated.

visual cortex   The region of the brain associated with processing visual information.

For More Information

ORGANIZATIONS

American Mental Health Association
191 Presidential Boulevard., Suite 3-W
P.O. Box 345
Bala Cynwyd, PA 19004
Web site: http://www.drmckenzie.com
e-mail: info@drmckenzie.com

Brain Injury Association USA
105 North Alfred Street
Alexandria, VA 22314
(703) 236-6000
Web site: http://www.biausa.org

Canadian Mental Health Association
Ontario Division
180 Dundas Street West, Suite 2301
Toronto, ON
MSG 1Z8 Canada
(416) 977-5580
e-mail: division@ontario.cmha.ca

The Dana Alliance for Brain Initiatives
745 Fifth Avenue, Suite 900
New York, NY 10151
Web site: http://www.dana.org/about/dabi
e-mail: danainfo@dana.org
A nonprofit organization that provides information about the
    benefits of brain research.

National Mental Health Association
1021 Prince Street
Alexandria, VA 22314-2971
(703) 684-7722
Web site: http://www.nmha.org

WEB SITES

Due to the changing nature of Internet links, the Rosen Publishing
Group, Inc., has developed an online list of Web sites related to the
subject of this book. This site is updated regularly. Please use this
link to access the list:

http://www.rosenlinks.com/lfm/rehb/

For Further Reading

Brynie, Faith. *The Physical Brain.* Woodbridge, CT: Blackbirch Press, Inc., 2001.

Cobb, Vicki. *Feeling Your Way: Discover Your Sense of Touch.* Brookfield, CT: Millbrook Press, 2001.

Edelson, Edward. *The Nervous System.* Farmington Hills, MI: Chelsea House Publishers, 1989.

Marvis, B. *Smell.* Farmington Hills, MI: Chelsea House Publishers, 1995.

Marvis, B. *Taste.* Farmington Hills, MI: Chelsea House Publishers, 1995.

Parker, Steve. *The Brain and Nervous System.* Danbury, CT: Franklin Watts, 1991.

Roca, Nuria Bosch. *The Nervous System, Our Data Processor.* Farmington Hills, MI: Chelsea House Publishers, 1995.

Royston, Angela. *Thinking and Feeling.* Portsmouth, NH: Heinemann Library, 1997.

Silverstein, Alvin. *The Nervous System.* Brookfield, CT: Twenty-First Century Books, 1995.

Wilkinson, Beth. *Coping When a Grandparent Has Alzheimer's Disease.* New York: The Rosen Publishing Group, Inc., 1995.

Bibliography

Davidoff, Jules, ed. *Brain and Behavior: Critical Concepts in Psychology.* New York: Routledge, 2000.

Druckman, Daniel, and John I. Lacey. *Brain and Cognition: Some New Technologies.* Washington, DC: National Academy Press, 1989.

Gupta, Ayodhya, ed. *Arthropod Brain: Its Evolution, Development, Structure and Functions.* New York: Wiley, 1987.

Llinas, Rodolfo R. *The Biology of the Brain: From Neurons to Networks.* New York: Freeman, 1989.

Newton, Thomas, and D. Gordon Potts, eds. *Advanced Imaging Techniques.* San Anselmo, CA: Clavedel Press, 1983.

Oakley, David A. *Brain and Mind.* New York: Methuen, 1985.

Index

A

Alzheimer's disease, 8, 21–22, 24, 25, 27
anxiety disorders, 15, 18–21, 37, 48
  causes of, 20
  treating, 20–21
artificial intelligence, 7, 51, 55
autoreceptor, 16, 18, 20
axon, 12, 24

B

brain, the
  ability to heal itself, 8–9
  about, 5–13, 30, 52, 55
  age and, 33–35, 37
  blood vessels and, 36
  cloning, 7
  computers and, 7, 10, 29–30, 51–53, 54
  drugs/alcohol and, 19
  the future and, 51–55
  intelligence/learning/ memory and, 8, 27–37, 55
  moral issues and, 7, 55
  sensory information and, 7–8, 9, 45–49
  sleep/dreams and, 39–43
  study/research of, 5–10, 11
  treating, 9–10
brain disorders, 9, 16–25
  classification of, 6
brain function
  controlling, 7, 53
  during sleep, 41
brain waves, measuring, 40

C

chemical imbalance, 15, 33, 48
cloning, 7, 25, 55
computers, thought-controlled, 52–53

D

dementia, 31
dendrite, 12–13
depression, 6, 15–18, 20, 21, 48
  causes of, 16
  treating, 6, 17–18

Credits

ABOUT THE AUTHOR

Jennifer Viegas is a reporter for *Discovery News* and is a features columnist for Knight Ridder newspapers. She also writes for ABC News, Physicians for Social Responsibility, the *Washington Post*, and other publications.

PHOTO CREDITS

Cover © Taro Yamasaki/TimePix; cover inset (front and back), p. 1 © PhotoDisc, Getty Images; folio banners © Eyewire; p. 4–5 © Pia Schachter/IndexStock Imagery; p. 6 © AP/Wide World Photos/Cyberonics, Inc.; pp. 8, 28, 40, 49 © BSIP Agency/Index Stock Imagery; p. 12 © BSIP/Giles/Photo Researchers; p. 14–15 © Jan Leethsa, MD/Custom Medical Stock Photo; p. 17 © BSIP/Jacopin/ Photo Researchers; pp. 23, 42 © SIU BioMed/CMSP; p. 26–27 © Cohen/CMSP; p. 36 © Art & Science/CMSP; p. 38–39 © BSIP/CMSP; p. 44–45 © Omikron/Photo Researchers; p. 46 © CMSP; p. 50–51 © Stephen Chernin/AP/Wide World Photos; p. 54 © AFP/Corbis.

DESIGN AND LAYOUT

Evelyn Horovicz